Poems In The Key of 'B

Faith, Family, & Love

Barbara S. Corley

B. Publishing

2024

ISBN: 979-8-218-41741-3 (Paperback)
ISBN: 979-8-218-41733-8 (eBook)

Book Design by Tamara L. Corley
Illustrations by Fleming Schofield (p.15)

JEHOVA SHALOM
"My Prince of Peace"

I dedicate this book to my Savior and King,
Jesus Christ, the Lover of my soul and the
Lifter of my head.

It is by His Grace that the gift of writing,
speaking, and poetry was given to me to use
to give Him the glory and to share my love for
Him and His creation.
He is my Counselor.
He is my Lord.
He is my Everything.

Thank You, Lord for Your mercies new every
morning and for this gift You have entrusted
me with.

FOREWORD

An outpouring of the Lord's words of
love and inspiration from His lips to my
heart to these pages. I wrote these
poems to inspire faith in God and love
for mankind.

TABLE OF CONTENTS

Coming Out

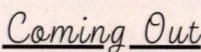

I'm walking alone, stumbling at times;
Walking in darkness where there seems to be no end.
I'm searching and reaching, reaching for light;
There's an end to this tunnel and I'm coming out.
My journey seems long, but I can endure;
My patience won't waiver,
I'll stand on my faith.
I'll fight the good fight,
Because I'm coming out.
No more stumbling in the dark,
No more groping for the light.
My heart is open to God's word,
And I'm coming out.
My hand is in His hand,
My love for Him is strong.
His light in me shines bright,
And I'm coming out.

Don't Give Up

Don't give up, God is near
He will always meet you there.
You say, "Where is 'there'?"
It's anywhere you are,
He is always near.
You say, "But my knowledge of God
Is not very strong.
I have done so many things
That I knew was wrong.
I wasn't asking for His guidance
I just did things on my own.
Now I'm in this valley and I feel so alone.
All I can think of are the things I did wrong.
If I call on Him now, will He hear my cry?"
Yes, He will my child, as I told you before
He is always standing by.
So, lift up your voice, pour out your heart.
Tell Him you mean it
When you promise to never again depart.
He will hear your prayer and answer your call.
True to His word, He will never let you fall.

Give Thanks

I know we all like to say, "When I woke up this morning…"
But wait, think about it, then you should say,
"God woke me up this morning. So, I give Him thanks
That He blessed me to be here for another beautiful day.
As we start on our journey today,
Whether it's to work or to play, We should all say,
"Father, please Go with me and guide me all the way".
How many of you know that the job you have,
God gave it to you?
The family you love and enjoy, He gave you them too.
And don't forget the house and the car.
What, say that again?
Yes, it was our Father in Heaven
Who took you near and far.
So be grateful and say,
"God Almighty, I thank You for making a way,"
His word says that we are all like the grass that withers away.
So, without His hand holding us
Where would we be at the end of the day?
So, remember to say, "Thank You Lord, It's to You I pray".
And, brothers and sisters, don't let your minds go blank,
When it's time to give thanks.
Say it in private, say it out loud
Let our Father in Heaven know
And you will make Him proud.

God's Majestic Creations

I am happy and singing, as I swing in the breeze.

Admiring God's Majestic Creations,

The birds, the flowers and, the trees.

The birds are the first sound I hear,

When He wakes me up each morning.

Singing in such beautiful melodies

As they perch in the trees.

They seem to be saying, "Awake, it's a new day,

Come sing with me, let's fly away."

The trees are just awesome, so majestic in height.

They are home for the birds, when they're not in flight.

Their arms are stretched wide, as if

reaching for the clouds.

Their leaves give them character from

spring through fall.

They grow and change colors and I love and enjoy it all.

When I look at the flowers, they put my mind at ease.

So many beautiful colors,

Like waves of freshness swaying in the breeze.

Some short, some tall,

So many different kinds, I can't begin to name them all.

OH GOD, HOW MAJESTIC ARE YOUR CREATIONS!!!.

<u>Let Love Have Its Way</u>.

If I told you today that I love you,
Would you turn and walk away?
Or, would you feel my love and stay?
If I said to you, "Let love have its way."
Would you trust me then?
Or, would you ponder it in your heart
While trying to figure out exactly,
What you want to say?
If you told me that you loved me,
I would look deep into your eyes.
It would take me only a moment
Before I knew for sure.
Then I would know exactly what to say,
Which would be, "Let love have its way."
If you love someone, and you know it's real.
It shouldn't be hard to say.
Just tell them how you feel.
Say it from your heart,
And Let love have its way!!!

<u>Looking Through The Mirror</u>

Reflections of the future,
What do you see?
The glory of God shinning down on me;
Saying, "Hearken to My voice,
Reach for My shining light,
Step out on faith, you'll be alright".
Reach out for wisdom,
She's crying out for you.
Hold on to instruction,
You will need that too.
Mount them on your mirror
So each day you'll see,
The reflections of both
Wherever you may be.
Pray for understanding
To go with the two,
So you'll know what to do
When God gives them to you.
Hold out I say!
And wait on the three;
For if you don't get them,
You will never be free.

Mother

She holds you in her arms,
She tells you it's going to be alright.
When she says, "I Love You",
The look on her face tells you it is TRUE.
When You can go to her with your dreams,
Watch how her face BEAMS!
When they don't work out,
and You go to her with your tears,
She calms and quiets all of your fears.
She says, "It's going to be alright.
Don't give up just because that dream
Didn't work out right.
Reach higher next time and Trust in God,
He will always show you the LIGHT!!!"
Who is this woman
That teaches you what is so right?
Don't tell me you haven't figured it out?
She is one like no other,
She is YOUR MOTHER.

Quiet Times

A cool breeze, a thought of long ago,

Soft music,

Pictures of a face in my head that I cannot let go.

A meadow of flowers

With all the colors of a rainbow.

Etched in my mind with the passing of time.

The glistening dew in the hours before dawn

Have fallen on blades of grass

And petals of dandelions.

A falling leaf, a bird singing in the distance,

Triggers memories of a past

To which I have no resistance.

Remembrance of a love song from days long past,

Stirs thoughts of a relationship that just did not last.

I lose myself to the joy of it all,

And the peace I feel, Only God can reward.

It's quiet times like these

When I feel the pain and the joy,

When I realize that life's pleasures

Are not just a toy.

The Gift of Love

It can't be wrapped and given in a box,
It can't be held back for special occasions.
It has to be given every day, every hour,
It's the gift that has so much power.
Sometimes it's accepted, sometimes it's not,
It's often misused and then forgotten.
It causes hurt, sometimes shame.
What is this gift? Love is its name.
It's often abused for a mere lack of sensitivity,
By those who think it's just a small thing.
While the one who's giving it feels so much pain.
Sometimes we hesitate to bring out this gift.
We try hard to pretend that it just doesn't matter.
But oh how we yearn to let it overflow,
Hoping that the receiver will somehow know.
But this gift is like a dove, what is this gift?
It's the gift of love.

<u>Under Your Shadow</u>

When I was little, I sat on your knee.
You told me then
What a great person I would grow up to be.
When I got a little older,
You taught me to pray.
You said, "That's what we do
Each and every day."
When I started school,
you taught me to read.
It wasn't very easy
But I followed your lead.
The Bible verses you taught me,
I said them in class each day.
Everyone thought I was so smart,
Quoting from the Bible that way.
As I grew older, I saw other teens
Who were doing bad things,
And stuff that wasn't clean.
I wondered about it,
But I couldn't figure it out.
So, I asked you to tell me
What it was all about.
I wanted to know why I was this old,
and I didn't know about such things.
You said, "My child it's because
you were raised
Under the shadow of His wings."

When Love Calls

When love calls, don't try to run away.
You won't get very far, so you may as well stay.
Don't try to resist, what you should do is this,
Open your heart and revel in its bliss.
Lord, I wasn't searching for love
When You brought us together;
But here we are today, with a
Love that will last forever.
When love calls, you can't run away.
Your mind may be saying, "Go",
But your heart is telling you to stay.
I tried to run away on more than one occasion;
My feet were moving but my heart wasn't playing.
It let me know that it was staying.
In the beginning it was two, today we are four;
We followed our hearts and we decided to stay.
Because You're in our midst, each and every day,
Our love is strong and it will stay that way,
Our family's love is like steel, no pretenses, no deals.
See the smiles on our faces, they are real.
So here we are today, me, my wife and two kids.
Love called, and we answered.

Age

Don't worry about your age,
It's just a number.
Think about what you've come through,
And it will make you wonder.
Cherish each birthday as a gift from God.
If it were not for Him
You wouldn't have made it this far.
Don't let others tell you how you should look,
Or how you should dress.
You're a child of The Most High,
You always look your best.
People will always try
To put you to the test.
Just tell them Whose you are,
And that He looks at the inside,
Not at what you wear.
Maybe they will hear
and try Him for their selves.
Beauty comes with age
And you wear it well.
That beautiful smile on your face,
It says that He loves you
And crowns you with His grace.

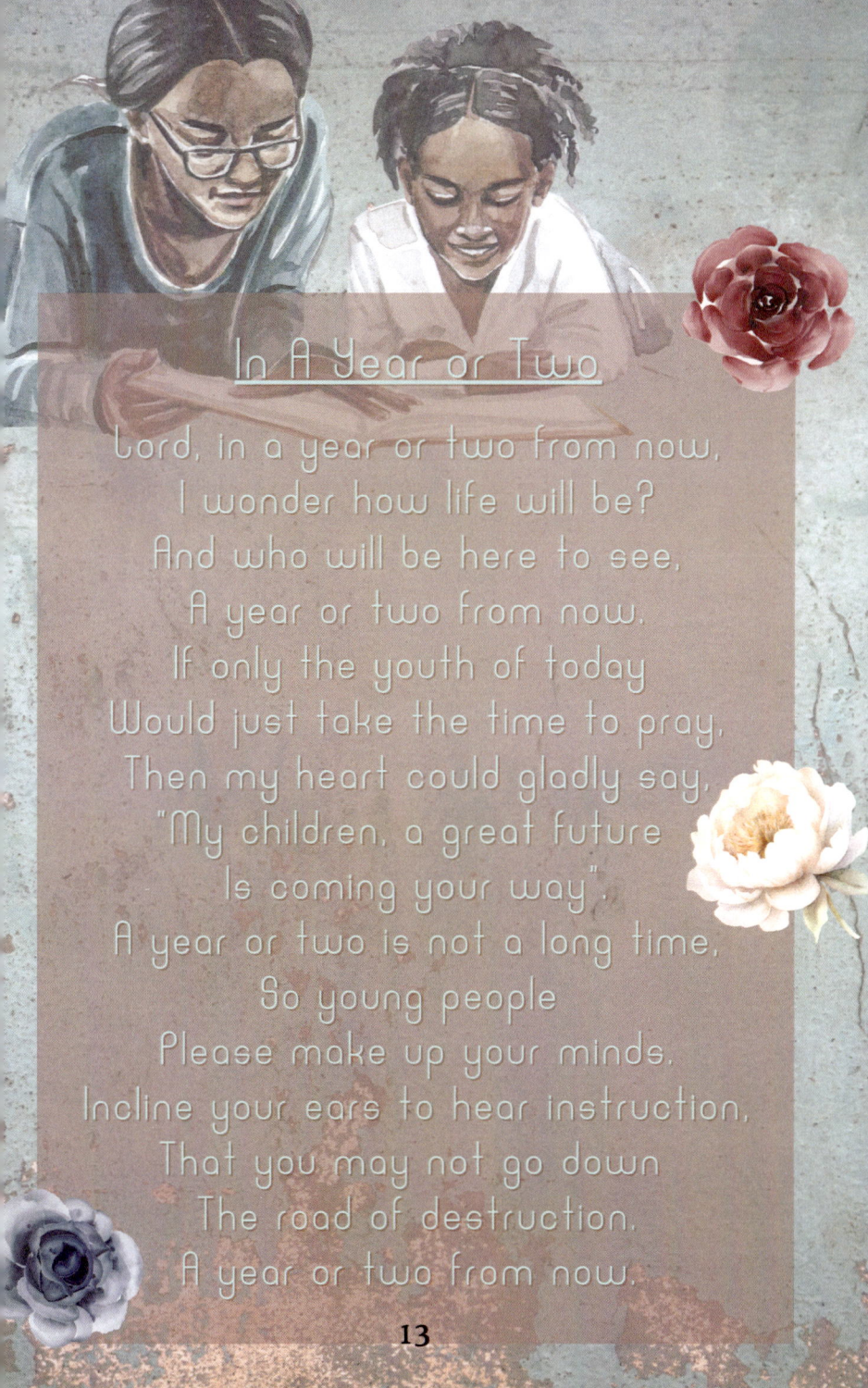

In A Year or Two

Lord, in a year or two from now,
I wonder how life will be?
And who will be here to see,
A year or two from now.
If only the youth of today
Would just take the time to pray,
Then my heart could gladly say,
"My children, a great future
Is coming your way".
A year or two is not a long time,
So young people
Please make up your minds.
Incline your ears to hear instruction,
That you may not go down
The road of destruction.
A year or two from now.

13

<u>Words</u>

I know there's a saying:
"Words cannot hurt"
But let me tell you
That is far from the truth.
I've been there and I've felt the pain
Of when words were used
To try to put me to shame.
When someone calls me names
And tries to put me to shame,
I scream and holler, Calling on God's name.
Because I know He's the only One
Who can heal my pain.
You don't tell your best friend
You don't want her to know.
And since the scars are on the inside
You think they don't show.
But let me tell you, that is wrong also.
Your closest friend, she'll always know
Because to her, your scars do show.
When you're going through the pain
The hurt and the shame
There are others out there
Who have been through the same.
And believe it or not, They too can see your pain.
So, don't shut yourself down,
Thinking there is no way out.
Talk to someone who will hear you out.
You may think that you have broken me
But I'm strong, I will not crumble.
So, you can come at me with your words full blast
But I stand on The Rock
And He won't let me stumble.

Move Forward

Don't stand there looking back.
Don't dwell on the "What If's".
Look ahead to tomorrow
Forget all those past sorrows.
Trust in God, He wants you to move forward.
The past is behind you, so give it a rest.
Move on toward your future no matter what the test.
Dwell on His word and you will have the best.
Look for the light that is shining so bright.
Trust and believe, then you will win the fight.
Begin to move forward, you will be alright.
Where you are now is not where you're meant to be.
Do you want to know why?
Because God has given you the Victory!
So, wake up your mind, wake up your soul.
Don't wait for tomorrow.
God wants you to Move Forward!